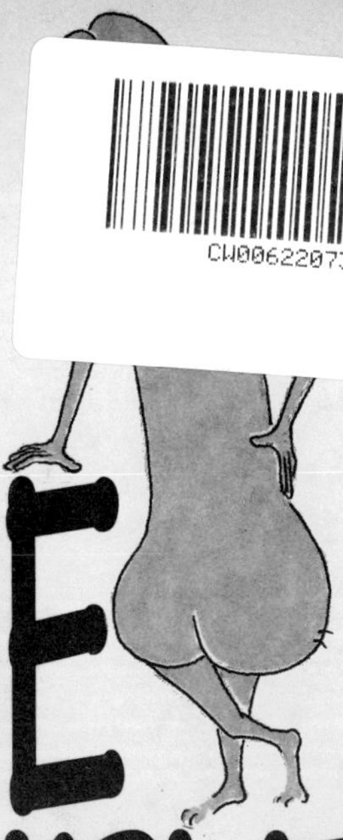

THE
COMPLETE
DICK

THE COMPLETE DICK

by

BOB GIBBS

WARNER BOOKS

A Warner Book

First Published in Great Britain in 1993 by Warner Books

A CIP catalogue record for this book is
available from the British Library.

ISBN 0 7515 0783 0

Printed and bound in Great Britain at
The Guernsey Press

Warner Books
A Division of
Little, Brown and Company (UK) Limited
165 Great Dover Street
London SE1 4YA

PREFACE

Having just made love to what he considered 'perfection', the man looked down at his organ of pleasure whilst relieving himself and quoted: 'If only you had brains, you'd rule the world.'

With this in mind we see no reason why a 'dick' cannot, indeed, have a life of its own - hence the following portrayal.

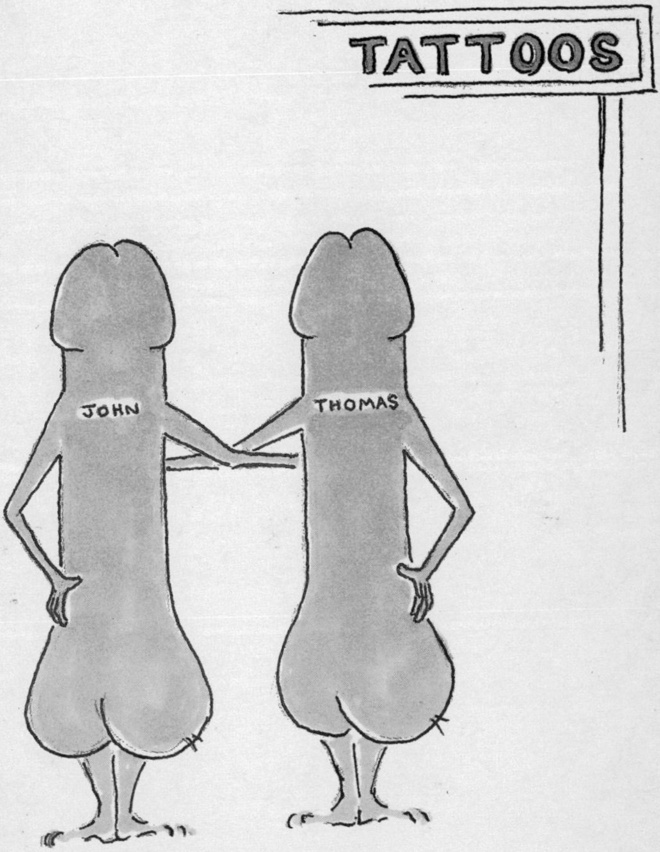
TATTOOS
JOHN
THOMAS

DICK BARTON - THE PRIVATE DICK

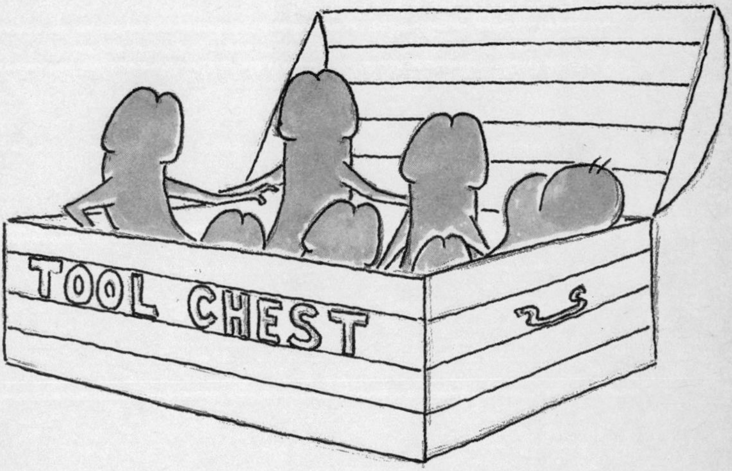
TOOL CHEST

ENJOYING A PISS UP WITH THE BOYS

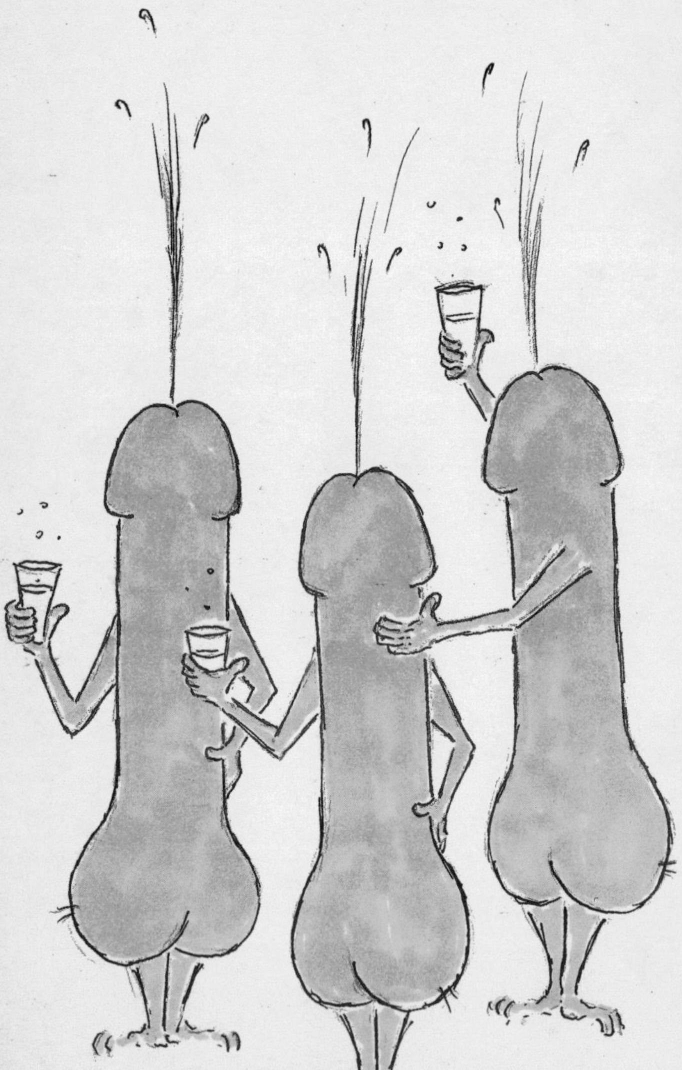

THE VENTRILOQUIST

BIG BOY
DILDO.

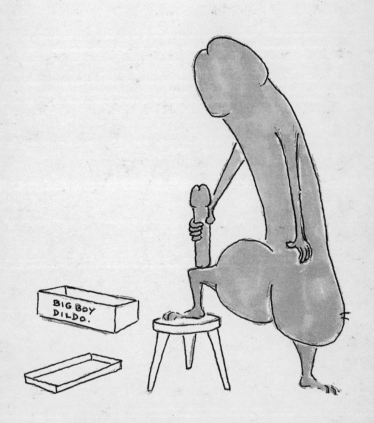

ORGAN DONOR

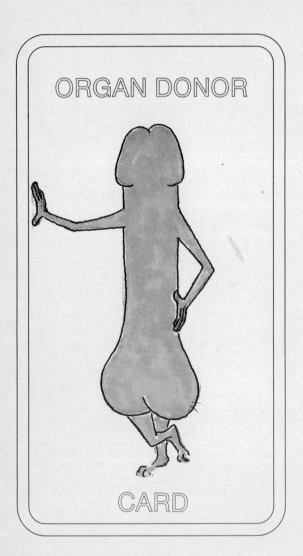

CARD

USING A DICKTAPHONE

SPOTTED DICK

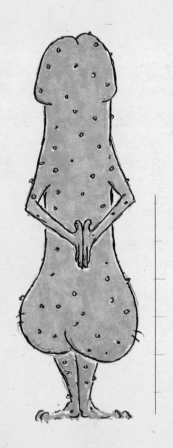

SMART DICK ABOUT TOWN

PETER O'TOOLE

DICK HEAD

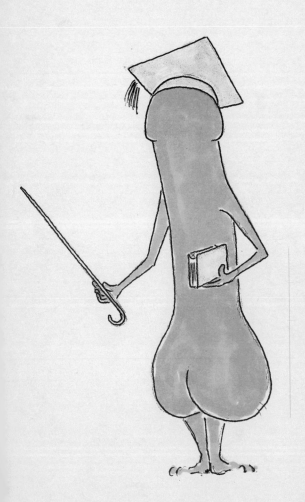

DISMEMBER

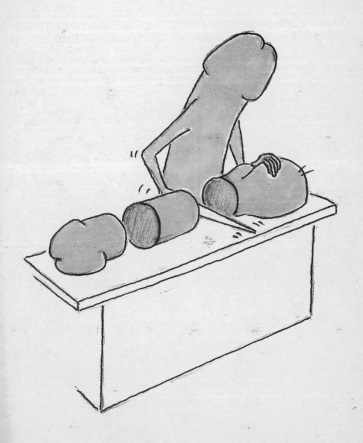

ERECTION HIRE
SERVICE
PEN 15

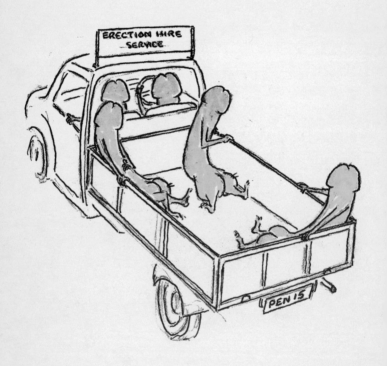

PRICKING OUT

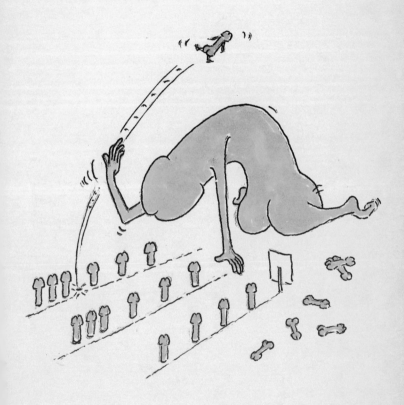

TOOL SHARPENER

COCKFIGHT

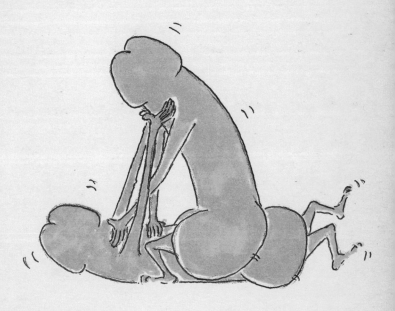

COCKPIT

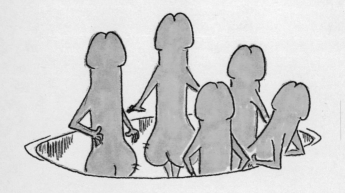

COCKNEY

NETBALL

COCKIELEEKIE SOUP

CONCOCKTION

SUPER DICK

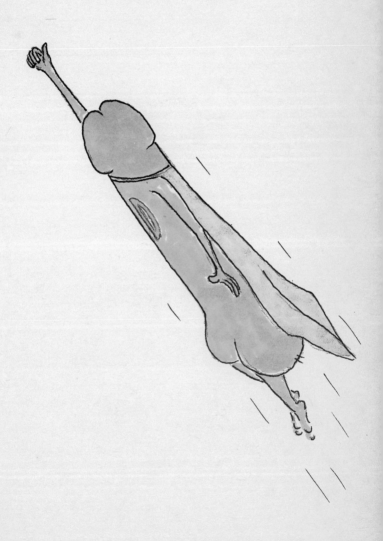

HAND BALL

A DICKY BIRD

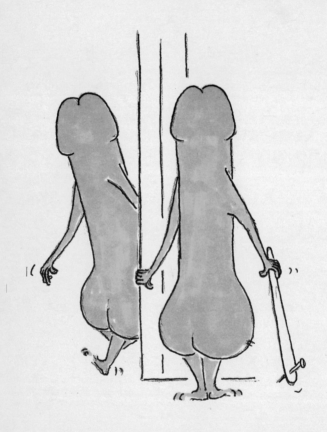

VINDICKTIVE

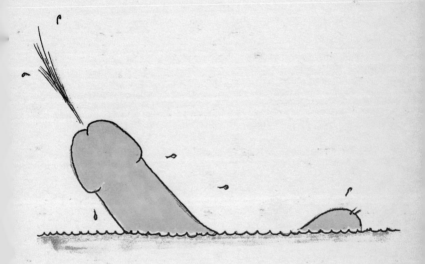

MOBY DICK

FEELING A LITTLE DICKIE

DICK TURPIN

PULLING A PLONKER

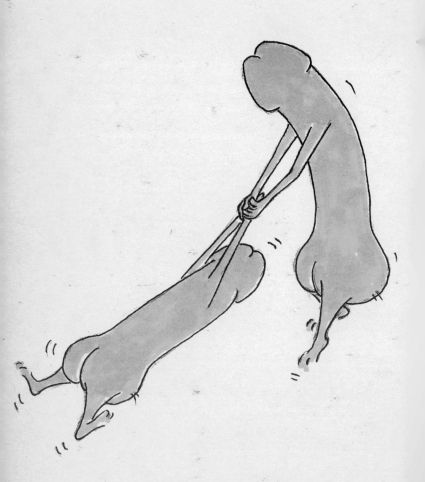

A FLASH PRICK

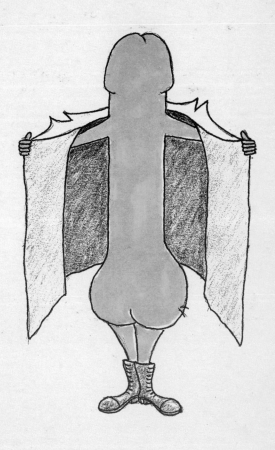

ORGAN LESSONS

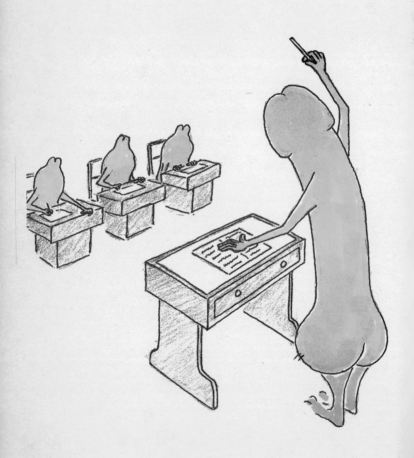

A BLOW JOB

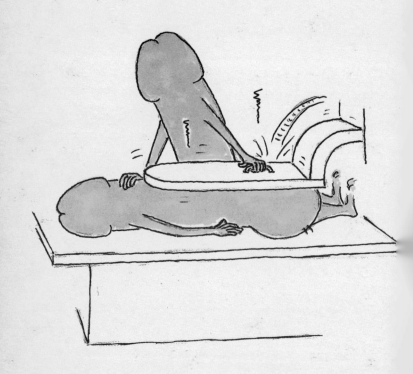

TOOL PRESS

PRIVATES

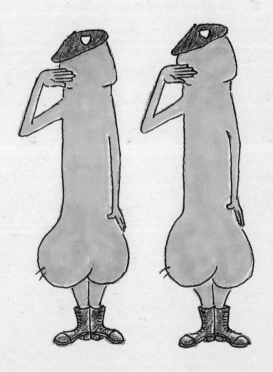

SHUTTLECOCK

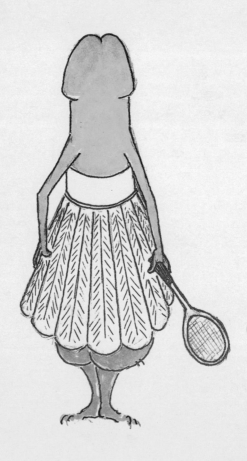

TOOL CUTTER

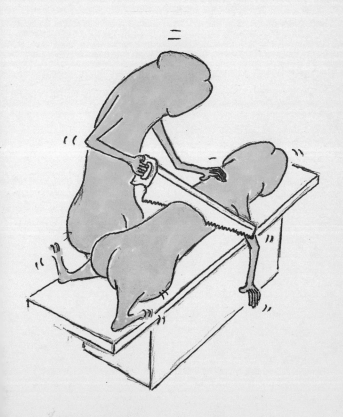

PERCY THROWER

DONG!

WATCH YA COCK!

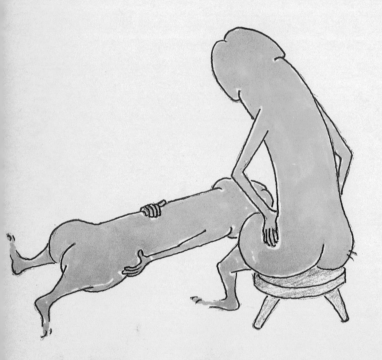

A COUPLE OF OLD PLONKERS

A BUNCH OF OLD PRICKS

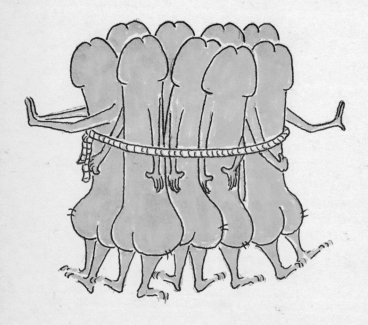

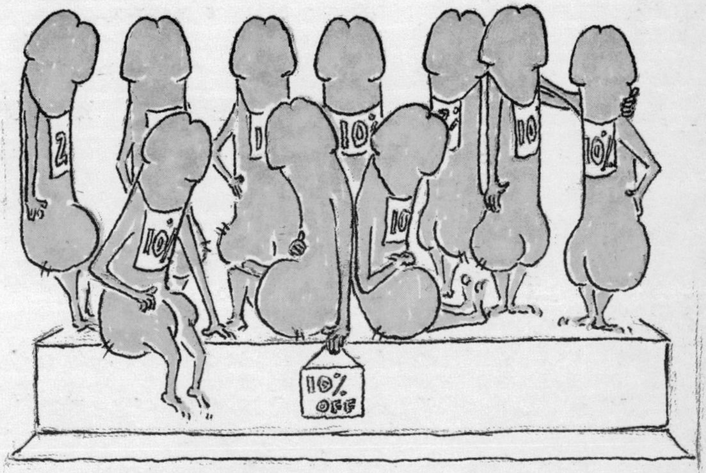
10% OFF

GRAND TOOL SALE

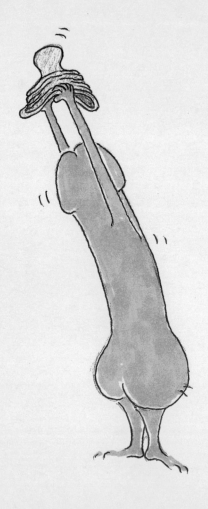

TAKING PRICK CAUTIONS

HIGH SPEED TOOL

RE MEMBER

KEEPING ONE'S PECKER UP

HERALDICK

MEMBER OF PARLIAMENT

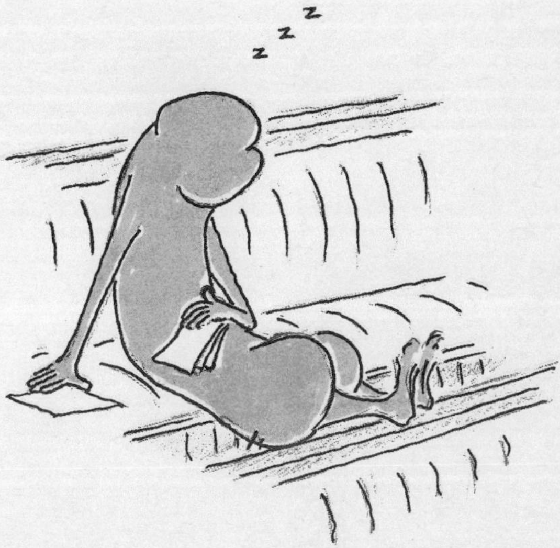
z z z

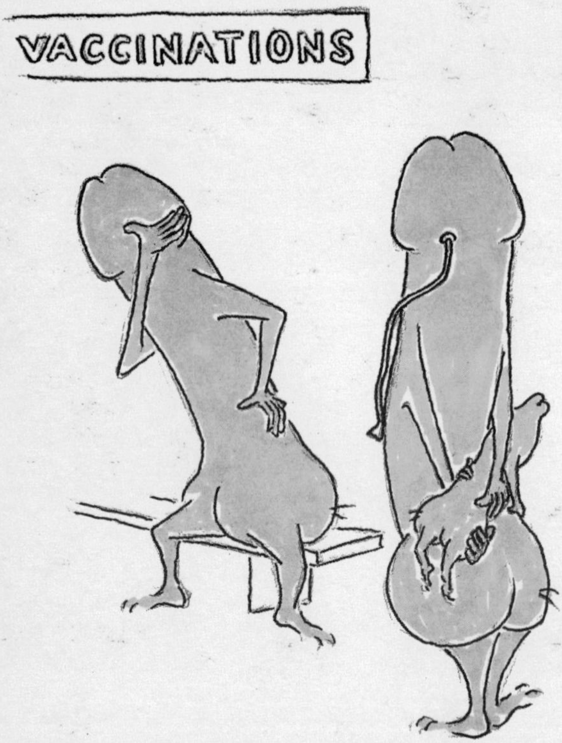
VACCINATIONS

'DON'T WORRY SIR - YOU'LL ONLY FEEL A LITTLE PRICK!'

UNDER MEDICKATION

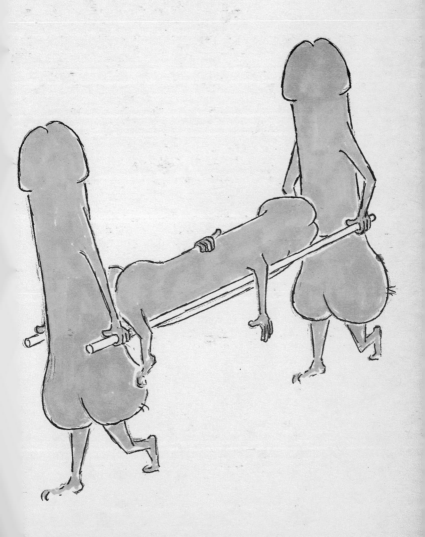

BENEDICKTINE MONK

z z z

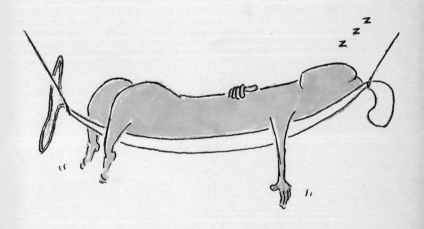

DOZY DICK

STUPID PRICK

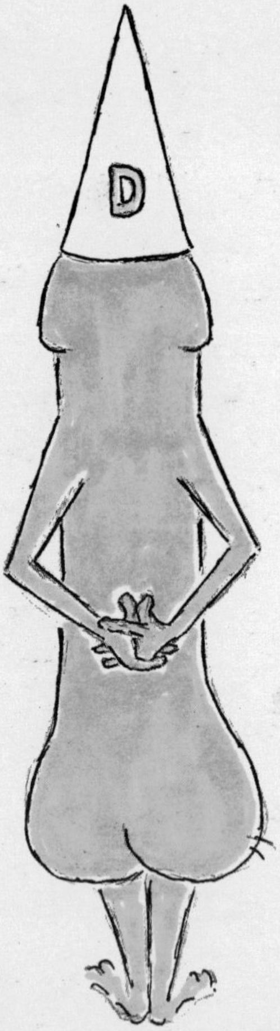
D

READING A DICKTIONARY

DICKSON OF DOCK GREEN

OUT B.B.B. - BOLLOCKS
BEFORE BALES

DICK TATOR

DICK WHITTINGTON

INDICKATOR

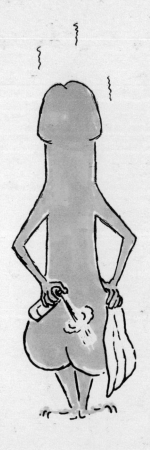

**PERSONAL HYGIENE AND
B.O. - BALL ODOUR**

SWEAT RASH CAN STRIKE
WITHOUT WARNING

PISSED OFF

PIRATE DICK AND HIS ...

... JOLLY ROGER

VASECTOMY - PRIVATE

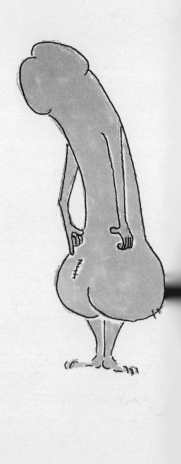

VASECTOMY - N.H.S.

FLIES ARE A SOURCE OF IRRITATION

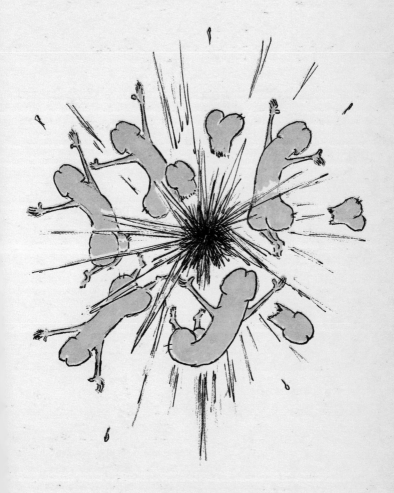

GANG BANG

A COCKTAIL

PROSTRATE?

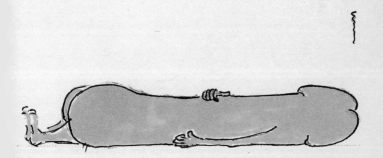

A KNOB

RIDICKULE

COCK A HOOP

WINNING PAIRS ROWING
TEAM WITH COX

VERDICKT

HAMPTON COURT

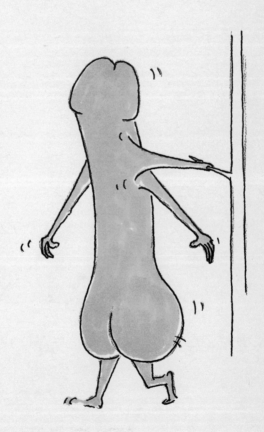

PERPENDICKULAR

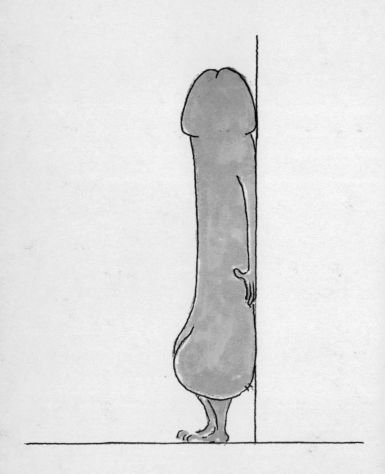

STOP COCK

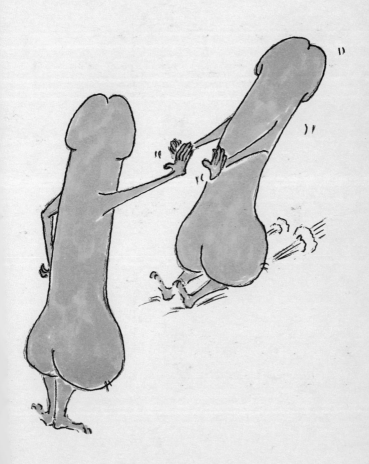

ORTHOPAEDICK

WOODCOCK

ACIDICK

POPPY COCK

COCKSURE

COCK UP

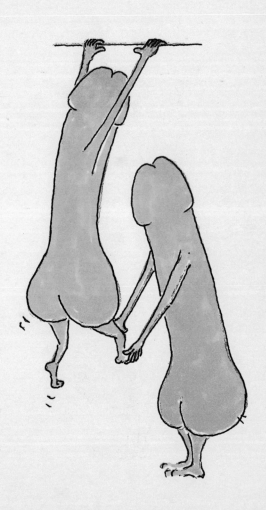

CUCKOO COCK

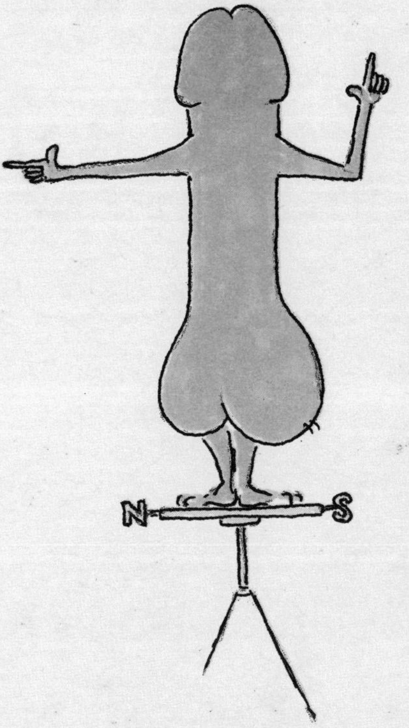
N
S

WEATHERCOCK

RICHARD III - DICK THREE

DICKY SEAT

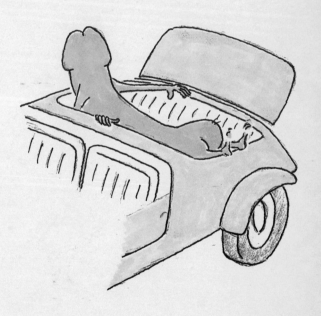

PRICKLY PEAR

WILD BILL HICKCOCK

SELF ABUSE

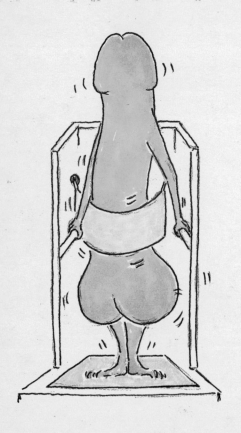

BALL BOY

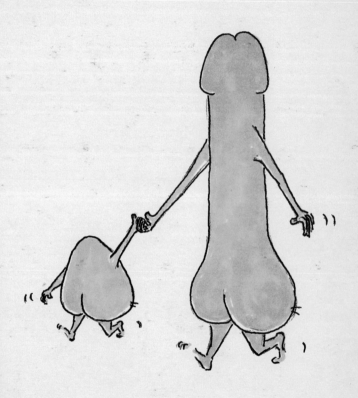

DICKENS

BREWER'S DICK

BALL COCK

COCK AND BULL STORY

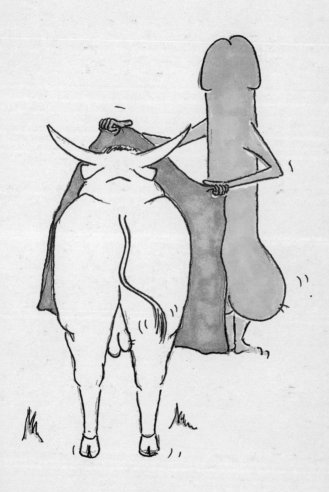

JIG TOOL

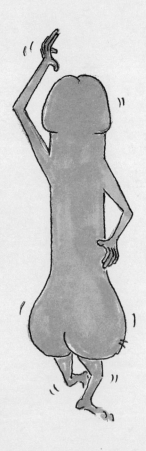

COCKY

DICKTUM

ORGAN GRINDER

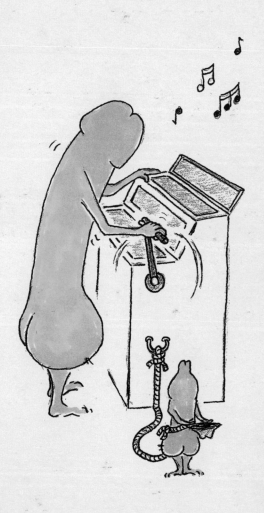

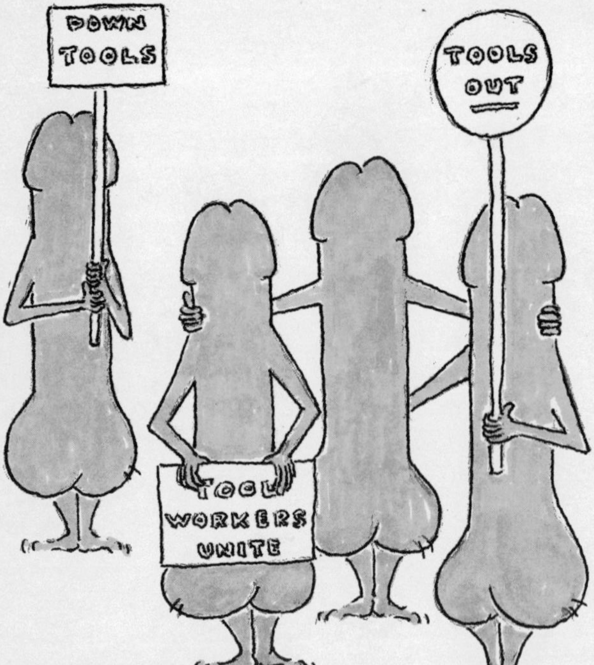
DOWN TOOLS
TOOL WORKERS UNITE
TOOLS OUT

TOOLS OF THE TRADE

FIGHTING OFF A DOSE OF CRABS

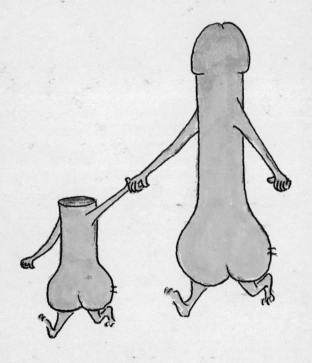

HALF COCKED

ORGANIST

POWER TOOL

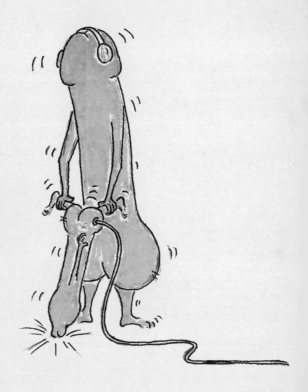

ALL TOOLED UP

KNOBBEE

TOOL MACHINIST

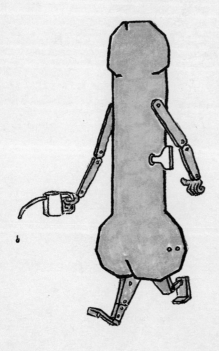

COCK EYED

DOWN TOOLS!

ERADICKATE

EDICKT

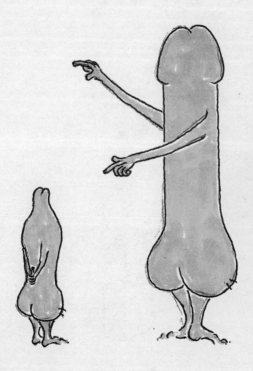

SPORADICK

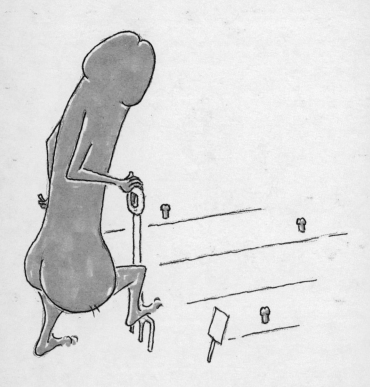

TOOL MOULDER

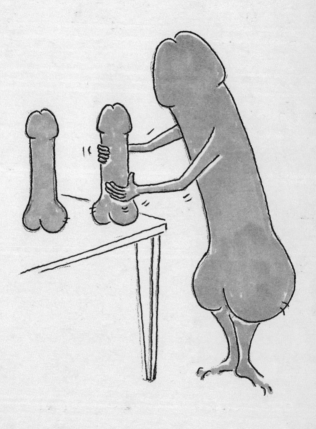

HAND TOOLS

ORGANISMS

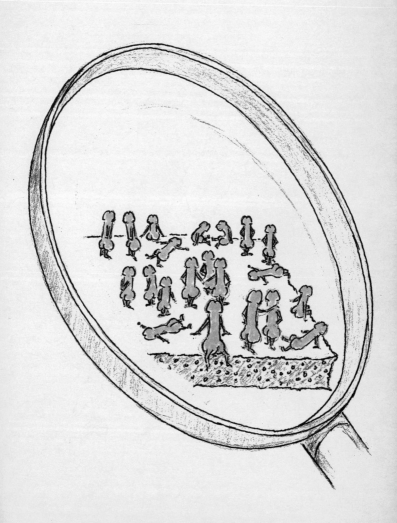

MEMBERSHIP

GLEN FIDDICK

BANGKOK

MELODICK